Guided Meditation for Detachment from Overthinking, Anxiety, and Depression

Beginner Friendly Meditations to Help You Reduce Anxiety, Relax Deeply and Become Free from Overthinking

Table of Contents

Introduction

When your thoughts and actions get tainted by negative images and feelings of unease, it is easy for stress, fear, anxiety, and even depression to swoop in. To close the door to these unwanted sensations, and stop yourself from boarding the never-ending vicious journey of overthinking and distress, you need to train your mind and body to detach, get distracted, and fall into a state of total calmness.

Through this 5-hours-worth of meditation, you allow me to guide you back to safety, whenever you feel anxious. Together, we will create a world of peace and serenity, where you can escape to when the shadow of negativity darkens your days.

Whether you are suffering from depression, have frequent anxiety attacks, or cannot stop your racing mind from replaying unwanted thoughts and images over and over again, this book will guide your way to calmness and help you find comfort and peace in no time.

By practicing these carefully-created meditation scripts regularly, you will not only boost your mood and relax at that moment but will eventually battle these mental destroyers for good.

Now, find a comfortable spot, settle down, and let's travel where tranquility rules together!

General Mindfulness Anxiety Relieving Meditation (30 minutes)

Duration: 30 minutes

Welcome to this guided meditation that is an excellent tool for knocking down everyday tension and anxiety, but just as successful in helping you overcome some more stressful events in your life. Through this 30-minute meditation technique, we will train the mind to become mindful of the surroundings, alert, and present, which can be a beneficial release practice for when the tension piles up inside.

Before we begin, please, find a comfortable place to sit. Whether it is on the floor, on the chair, or your fancy meditation pillow, it doesn't matter. The important thing is for you not to feel any discomfort during this practice.

Turn off your phone and other electronics, and minimize distractions.

Now, sit comfortably and close your eyes.

As we start, let's take a moment to check on your feelings and sensations. This mindful check of your mind and body is an essential starting point, so make sure not to skip this step. Feeling and acknowledging the sensations and whatever thoughts and emotions overflow you will help you realize what you need to guide your attention from. Now, check your mood, body tightness, thoughts, and emotions, acknowledge what is felt, and just let be.

Very gently, withdraw from your feelings and thoughts, placing your attention on your breath only. Slowly, inhale deeply, noticing the tension and expanding of your abdomen. Breathe out, just as slowly, acknowledging how your stomach relaxes as the breath leaves your body.

Repeat. Breathe in and breathe out. Breathe in—breathe out. Keep breathing and keep your attention on the breath.

Notice how your abdomen rises with each breath you take, and how it falls when you breathe out.

Keep your attention on your breath for a couple more minutes.

Breathe in.

Breath out.

Breathe in.

Breathe out.

Focusing on our breath can help us calm down when anxiety overpowers our state of mind, so make sure that you breathe with awareness to master this practice.

If you notice that a sudden feeling or unwanted thoughts have interrupted the silence – it is okay. Do not judge yourself for slipping. You are only human. It is in our nature to think and feel. You cannot shut your mind off, so don't try to make it blank – you cannot. Instead, be compassionate about your thoughts and feelings, make a mental note that they are there, but do not let them run this show. You are behind the wheel, and you choose which way you want to go. And right now, you want to go back to your breath.

Breathe in.

Breathe out.

Breathe in.

Breathe out.

You have the power to control what you decide to put your attention on. Notice how breathing deeply feels in your nostrils, abdomen, imagine your lungs expanding and shrinking with every inhale and exhale.

Breathe in.

Breathe out.

Let's move the attention to your body now. By doing this so-called body scan, you become more in-tune with your feelings, more alert of your sensation, and more present in this moment.

Let's start at the bottom and work our way up. Bring your attention to your feet. If your feet are on the ground, feel the soles by applying mild pressure. How do your feet feel? Notice the toes, the bottom of the feet, and do your best to place every shred of attention there. It is essential to try to really feel.

Now, move the attention up to your ankles, your calves, your shins, rising up all the way to your knees. Notice how this part of your body feels and gently move upwards. Feel your upper legs, your hips, the pelvic area. Now, you're at the center of your body. Be aware and notice the sensations. Do you feel tightness? Does some part ache? Is there any tension?

If you can loosen up a little bit and relax any tight parts, now is the time to do it. If you cannot do it, it is okay. Do not judge. Remember, just let be.

As you move toward the spine, back and shoulders, do the same. Be aware of how your body feels. If you can soften some areas and help yourself relax, it is vital to do so.

Move your attention to your chest now, letting your focus go up to the sternum, your ribs... Take a deep breath and notice how your chest puff up. How does this feel? As you breathe out, slowly shift the attention back to your shoulder blades. Be aware of how they connect to your neck, and move upwards.

Feel the neck, throat, jaw… Let the awareness go up to your cheeks, temples, forehead. Acknowledge your facial structure and make sure to feel into each part. Feel your whole head and face with awareness. Your eyes are closed. Note how the lids feel. Are they heavy and tense? Are you beginning to relax?

Gently, start moving the awareness downwards, toward your feet. Slowly, turn your attention to your neck again. Feel the connection to the shoulders; see how your shoulder blades feel. Feel your arms, chest, your abdominal area. Move down to your hips, pelvic, upper legs, knees, until you reach the feet again. Feel your whole body as a whole, from your head down to your toes.   If something feels tight or tense, stretch or move your body gently to loosen up. Remember, you should feel relaxed and comfortable in your own body.

As you are scanning your body, you may notice your anxious feelings and thoughts piling up again. That's okay. Let them be. Acknowledge that they are there - let the stress, fear, or whatever undesired emotions you are experiencing, be.

Imagine that you are inside the comfort of your warm home. Now, all of a sudden, you leave the house. But it is so cold outside, freezing. You may be hit with a temperature shock at first, but as time passes, your body becomes more and more accustomed to the cold. Your anxiety is just like that cold. It may be intense and severe at first, but acknowledging those thoughts and feelings and just letting them be, will knock down the power they hold over you. Your body and mind will slowly get used to them. Feeling into your anxiety and fears will help you become mindful of how you feel. And being mindful will eventually help you win the anxiety battle. Be compassionate and do not judge. It is okay to feel this anxious. It is okay to have these thoughts.

Now, very gently, detach from your feelings and thoughts. Take a deep breath and try to focus on your breathing.

Breathe in.

Breathe out.

Breathe in.

Breathe out.

If it takes you a while to detach and cannot immediately shake off the anxiety within, that's okay. Take your time to move your attention to the way you breathe slowly. Do not judge. You have all the time in the world. This is not a competition, nor something set in stone. Remember, you are in control. You make the rules. Do it at your own pace.

Breathe in.

Breathe out.

Breathe in.

Breathe out.

Move your awareness to your abdominal area. Notice how your chest feels – acknowledge the rise and fall with every inhale and exhale. Breathe in deeply – puff up and tense. Breathe out slowly – release and relax.

Repeat. Breathe in – tighten. Breathe out – relax.

Take a deep breath – you feel your chest puff up, your abdomen tightens, the tension piling up in this area.

Breathe out very slowly through your nose – you feel the chest deflate, the tightness gradually turns into relaxation – the tension into a feel-good sensation.

Inhale deeply – feel the air that goes into your nostrils.

Exhale – acknowledge how the release of the breath makes you feel more relaxed.

Breathe in – tighten.

Breathe out – relax.

Breathe in – tighten.

Breathe out – relax.

Focus on your breathing for a minute.

Do not judge yourself if anxious thoughts creep in and disrupt your silence again. It is okay to have them. It is okay to feel. It is okay to be in-tune with your emotions. It is also okay to choose not to allow them to affect you. Notice that the thoughts are there, but do not allow them to occupy your mind. Do not overthink whatever has been bothering you. Continue breathing. Breathe in. Breathe out.

Imagine yourself detaching from your thoughts and emotions. Imagine you leaving them behind you as you slowly move forward.

Breathe in.

Breathe out.

Your anxiety is behind you now. You've escaped your fears. You are safe.

Move your awareness back to your breath. Inhale deeply. Exhale and relax.

Inhale.

Exhale.

Continue breathing deeply.

You are moving forward and leaving your fears and undesired emotions behind. There is nothing but happiness and feelings that make you feel good inside you now. Imagine yourself looking back as you move forward. The anxiety gets smaller and smaller until it becomes a tiny spot you can barely even see. How can something so small overpower you? You choose not to be affected. You choose to be free.

As we move toward the end of the practice, take a moment to congratulate yourself on choosing to take control. Breathe in. Breathe out.

10. 9. 8.

We are moving toward the finish.

7. 6. 5.

Be present.

4. 3. 2. 1.

Open your eyes. You are here in this moment, present. You are safe. When you are fully alert, go back to your daily activities, trying to stay safe and calm.

Overcoming Overthinking and Obsessive Thoughts Guided Meditation (30 minutes)

Duration: 30 minutes

Welcome to this guided meditation that will help you distract yourself when obsessive or unhealthy thoughts take over your mind. With the help of this 30-minute practice, you will be able to stop the never-ending cycle of thoughts, anxiety, and even obsessive behavior for those suffering from OCD. Everyone who feels the need to let go of unwanted thoughts can benefit from this meditation. Whether it is a particular situation you cannot stop thinking about or an intense compulsive behavior that has been bothering you, through this practice, you will learn that you are pulling the strings. You are in control of your own mind.

Before we begin, make sure you are comfortable. If it is hot in your room, crack a window open. If it is colder, make sure the heating is on or that you are wearing warm clothes. The clothes you are wearing should also feel comfortable. This is important as even the tiniest discomfort can disrupt this practice.

Now, take a sit or even lie down if you are more comfortable that way. Close your eyes and keep your hands at your sides.

I am counting to five, and then you will find yourself in a different place.

1, 2, 3, 4, 5.

Now, imagine that you are somewhere dark and cold. It is not pleasant there. And you surely do not feel comfortable standing outside, in the cold. You are in a place where you shouldn't be. Surrounded by your unwanted thoughts, cloaked with anxiety. Imagine your thoughts going around, circling you. You want to break free from the cycle, but you do not know how to. As you are standing there with your anxiety and negative thoughts, take a moment to acknowledge them. Knowing what causes you to have these thoughts and feelings can help you escape them. Whatever has been troubling you, note that it's there, causing you distress.

As you are getting familiar with the destructive thoughts, you realize something. There is a way out of it. Imagine there is a road in front of you, and at the end of that road, there is peace, serenity, and total equilibrium. All you have to do to get there is to simply step out of the darkness and follow the path ahead.

Ánd that is exactly what you are doing at this moment. You are lifting one of your legs, and you are pushing your whole body ahead. You are now one step closer to that peaceful place. So, you take another step. And another. As you are slowly walking towards your destination of relaxation, you realize that each step you take is taking you to a warmer and better-lit place. You are no longer in the dark. You are no longer cold. It feels good to feel the sun warming your skin. It feels good to be walking away from something that has been causing you pain. It feels good to leave all of that behind.

Take another step. And another. Remember, each step you take gets you closer to a better place. And with each step, you are further away from your negative thoughts.

Now, you have reached the end of the road. It is warm and sunny; you can hear the birds chirping. You can hear a relaxing sound of water babbling. But you still don't see a river. You don't see the birds. All you see at this point is a large gate in front of you.

Imagine yourself grabbing the knob, but do not open the gate just yet. Feel the cold metal on your skin. Imagine how the knob feels in your hand.

Before you push it open, look back. The darkness of thoughts and destructive emotions are still circling in the distance, but they are so far away, you can barely see them. Acknowledge that you are allowing yourself to leave all negativity behind, and push the gate open.

Now, enter the equilibrium. It looks like everything you imagine heaven to be like. You can see the birds, the river, flowers, and butterflies. You can hear pleasant sounds. You feel safe at last. Safe and relaxed. You are so proud of yourself for getting away from your anxious thoughts.

Now, imagine yourself kicking off your shoes, and standing with your bare feet on the green grass. Feel the cold sensation that tickles your feet. Enjoy this moment. Safe and relaxed.

You are laying back, allowing the sun to warm your face. Your eyelids are closed, but you can see the light illuminating. You can feel the warmth hugging you. Embrace this feeling. Stay in this moment. Enjoy feeling this relaxed.

Just stay in that moment and breathe. Take a deep breath, and exhale slowly. Inhale and exhale.

Breathe in.

Breathe out.

Breathe in.

Breathe out.

Continue deep breathing and think about what it feels like to be free from the shackles of negativity. You can finally breathe freely. You are relaxed at last.

If your equilibrium gets interrupted by an urge to act on a compulsion, negative thought that has been bothering you, or something that you simply cannot get out of your head, it is okay. You may have allowed your mind to pull you back to the dark place where you are surrounded by anxiety and destructive thoughts, but you are still in the lead. You know the way out. You know of a safe place that is only yours. Your little heaven.

So, let's get back to that place together, shall we? Imagine yourself stepping out of the darkness again. Start walking toward the gate now, but this time, do it a little bit faster than the first time. Remember, you have just been there, you know the way. Take a step forward, and then another. And another. As you are walking towards your safe place, try to focus on the sensations along the way. Think about how it is getting warmer, how the sun is shining. As you are quickly moving towards the gate, it is getting warmer and warmer. You are feeling safer and calmer.

Now, you are at the gate again. Push it open and step inside. You are safe now. Alone and free from your thoughts. Shut the gate behind you and do not let your anxiety interrupt this blissful moment. Feel the positivity rising within. As the sun is getting warmer and warmer on your skin, you are feeling safer and safer. Your mind is at peace. Your body is relaxed. Be here, now, in this moment, and enjoy the serenity.

Take a deep breath and think about how lucky you are to be able to escape to such a beautiful place. Allow yourself to drift away. Breathing slowly. Breathing deeply.

Breathe in.

Breathe out.

Breathe in.

Breathe out.

As you breathe, try to imagine what is really like to be sitting barefoot in this lush meadow. Surrounded by colorful flowers. Inhale deeply and allow yourself to scent the flowery notes that are dancing in the air around you. Exhale slowly, focusing your mind on the beautiful sounds nature. Babbling. Chirping.

Breathe in – you are sniffing the flowers.

Breathe out – you are enjoying the sound that the river makes and admiring the birds.

Inhale.

Exhale.

Inhale.

Exhale.

If you allow an anxious thought to pop up, it's okay. If you are hit by a sudden rush to act on behavior, that's okay too. Just remind yourself that you are not your thoughts. You are not your compulsions. This negativity does not have any power over you. You are in control. You choose how to feel.

Now, acknowledge your thoughts and anxiety, but do not let them ruin this moment. They do not last forever. Your destructive thoughts are not facts. They are nothing more but images inside your head. Something that you do not want to engage in. Something that you need to let go.

Now, let yourself feel that negative energy that your never-ending thoughts drag with them. Do not get into details; just note how that feels. Know that it is there. It is not how you want to live your life. You do not want to be a slave to your anxiety. You wish to be free. You choose to be free. As you slowly start to detach from that feeling, you are transported back to your safe place. And as you see yourself floating to security and relaxation, you see the darkness of thoughts that you have left behind, getting shattered into million pieces. Your wish to be relaxed and positive is so strong that it managed to defeat the darkness inside your mind. Watch how those black pieces of unwanted thoughts, destructive emotions, and anxiety get lost in thin air. And as you watch them disappear, you realize how the meaning behind them gets lost, too. They become more meaningless and meaningless until finally, they lost all control over your mind. You are free. You are no longer trapped inside a maze of never-ending thoughts. Your mind is clear. You feel good. You are relaxed.

Sit down beneath a tree in the meadow, and imagine yourself gently caressing the fresh green grass with your hands. Try to feel the sensation the blades of grass bring to your palm. Stay in this relaxing moment and breathe.

Breathe in.

Breathe out.

Breathe in.

Breathe out.

5. Your mind is clear.

4. You are calm and deeply relaxed.

3. 2. 1.

Gently open your eyes. You have managed to stop the whirlwind of obsessive thoughts in your mind. Let's take a moment to congratulate yourself.

Slowly, become mindful of your surroundings, and gently stand up. Go back to your usual activities, and don't forget – only you control your mind.

Guided Meditation for Overcoming Stress-Related Anxious Feelings (30 minutes)

Duration: 30 minutes

If you are feeling anxious regarding an upcoming stressful event or you simply cannot put the past in the past and are constantly stressing over something that has already passed, this guided meditation will help you relax and teach you how to tame the stressful feelings. With this 30-minute meditation practice, you will be able to pause the stress, evaluate the situation, and realize that stressing over something and allowing anxiety to take over is only making things worse. This guided meditation will not only help you to calm yourself down when feeling distressed, but it will also clear your mind and help you come up with a healthy solution, faster.

First, make sure that you are free of distractions. Turn the TV and your phone off, close the window if there are distracting noises outside, and find a spot where you will be uninterrupted for about half an hour. Then, sit comfortably. The sitting position is not that relevant; what's important is for you to feel relaxed and comfortable. Close your eyes.

Let's start by performing a general relaxation technique. I will not count to 10, and you will breathe deeply, focusing on how the breath feels every time you inhale and exhale.

1, 2, 3, 4, 5, 6, 7, 8, 9, 10.

How are you feeling at this moment? Do the anxious feelings still overpower you? Or are you feeling more relaxed? Try to really get in-tune with your body. Notice your emotions and see how you are feeling, both mentally and physically. Are you in pain? Are you stressed? Are you tensed? Be aware of the state in which your entire body is at this moment, but do it without changing anything at this point. Just be aware.

Now that you know how you are feeling, let's shift your attention to your body by doing a quick body scan. This will help you distract yourself and knock down the intensity of the anxiety inside.

Starting with your feet, focus all of your attention there. How do they feel? Relax.

Now, slowly, go up to the ankles. See if there is any tension there. Relax.

Move upward, across the lower legs, check the knees, scan the upper thighs, and place your whole focus on your hips. Relax.

Check how your body feels at the pelvic area. Take a deep breath. Relax.

Keep scanning your bottom, abdomen, lower back. Relax.

Scan the middle back, go up to your chest, and take another deep breath. Is there any tension? See if you can soften it up. Relax.

Move toward the shoulders, scan your arms, elbows, wrists, hands. Relax.

Go back through the arms to the shoulders. How do your shoulder blades feel? Relax.

Move up to your neck, and start scanning your face. The mouth, jaw, cheeks, nose, forehead. Is there any tension? Is your face tight? Is your jaw clenched? Relax.

After scanning your head, slowly, start lowering your attention back toward your feet. Check your whole body to see if there is an area of tension, and do your best to relax. If needed, combine this with deep breathing if you think it will help you relax better.

Now, take a deep breath, and listen to me count. When I reach 30, you will have relaxed and released unwanted tension.

1, 2, 3, 4, 5, 6, 7, 8, 9, 10, 11, 12, 13, 14, 15, 16, 17, 18, 19, 20, 21, 22, 23, 24, 25, 26, 27, 28, 29, 30.

You are relaxed. There is no more tension. It feels good to be in your skin. Now that you are completely at ease, slowly transition into that stressful feeling again. You may think this is counterproductive, but your body and mind need to be exposed to such shock to get used to these feelings of uneasiness. Transitioning from *relaxed* to *stressed* will eventually train your mind to do the *stressed* to *relaxed* transition just as efficiently.

So, try to really think about what has been causing you stress and anxiety, and allow yourself to feel the emotions. Pinpoint the exact culprit of the stressful situation. Get really into it. Take your time, and go to the very beginning. When have you started having these feelings? What makes your heart racing and bursting with anxiety?

Maybe the stressor is obvious to you and you are dealing with a straightforward situation. Maybe it was a loss of some kind that gives you these feelings. Maybe it is fear of the unpredictability. Fear of the future. Fear of the unknown. Or perhaps you have trapped yourself in these thoughts and emotions, that it seems almost impossible to untangle and free yourself from this. Expose yourself to the situation you are trying to run away from, completely.

Take a deep breath. And another. And another. How does this make you feel? Is the anxiety severe? Are you afraid? Is your breath quickening? Take a mental note of the symptoms of stress and anxiety at this moment.

On a scale of one to ten, where ten is the most severe, how would you rate your feelings of stress and anxiety? What would it take for these feelings to become even more severe? Think about this for a while, and stay in the discomfort.

Breathe to 10, imagining yourself being wrapped with a cloak of anxiety that you do not know how to remove. Even if it is highly unpleasant and uncomfortable, stay with these negative feelings.

1, 2, 3, 4, 5, 6, 7, 8, 9, 10.

Are you severely anxious? Good. Note this moment, capture it mentally. Remind yourself that you allow yourself to feel this way, and yet, nothing bad has happened.

Now that you are stressed and anxous, let's try to relax ourselves again. To transition back to relaxation, imagine yourself getting on top of the situation. Whatever it is that you are dealing with, try to find a positive outcome. A solution to the problem that you are pleased with. If you have lost your job, think about finding a better one, one that pays a lot more, but still gives you more free time for yourself. Think about the things that bring you stress and anxiety, and create a scenario where you come up with a solution to your problems. The feelings of unease and fear no longer affect you.

Notice how you become less and less stressed. The anxiety is decreasing. The cloak of negativity is slowly letting go of your body. Allow yourself to enjoy the feeling of you finding a positive outcome to your stressful situations. Congratulate yourself for doing so. Take a moment to be proud of yourself for getting through these vicious emotions earlier. This practice only shows you that you are stronger than this. You are stronger than what your anxiety is trying to trick you into thinking.

Let's take this to an even more intense level. Now that you have found a positive outcome to the anxious situation, I want you to imagine yourself losing that feeling of comfort again. Think about that same stressful event happening all over again.

If you have lost your job and found a new one, now I want you to think about losing your new job, too. Think about your feel-good scenario getting shattered into pieces. I will not count to 5, and with each number, you will try to take your anxiety to a higher level.

1, 2, 3, 4, 5.

Now you have allowed stress to creep in again. Do you like this feeling? Of course, not. But did you find your previous transition to relaxation to be liberating? Then, let's get back to that serene place.

Again, imagine how it would feel for you to find a solution to this sudden stressful situation. Imagine yourself figuring a way out of this uncomfortable place. Think of a perfect solution – a scenario that helps you defeat the destructiveness once and for all. Now stay in this moment. Breathe deeply and enjoy the feelings of relaxation.

Breathe in.

Breathe out.

Breathe in.

Breathe out.

At last, you are at ease. Your head seems lighter, your body is free of tension. Your mind is clear, unaffected by negativity. You can think straight and make healthy, sane decisions.

Take a deep breath, and count to 10 with me, saying the numbers out loud. With each number, you become more and more aware that your stress and anxiety do not rule your life. You choose to be positive. You choose to find a solution to whatever it is that has been bothering you. You choose to live your life in peace. Relaxed and free.

1, 2, 3, 4, 5, 6, 7, 8, 9, 10.

Slowly open your eyes. Stretch your body gently, and get used to your surroundings.

You have survived some very intense feelings. Next time you practice this guided meditation, the anxious and stressful feelings will be less severe. With each practice, you will become better and better at controlling your emotions. This will train your mind to be better prepared for real-life stressors, and will also help you think clearly and focus your energy toward finding a solution.

Dealing with Anxious Images and Flashbacks (30 minutes)

Duration: 30 minutes

Sometimes we are revisited by something unpleasant that happened in the past. These flashbacks of unwanted situations, feelings, or events, can disrupt our day-to-day life, dragging fears, anxiety, and all sorts of negativity with them. This 30-minute guided meditation practice will help you remember to stay in the present and re-focus yourself on something positive.

You can practice this meditation when such images and flashback find their way into your mind, or you can also do it when you are not affected by negativity, to train your mind to embrace positivity, and let go of the dark side of the past.

For starters, find a comfortable place where you can sit and not be interrupted for about half an hour or so. Minimize distractions and make sure you are comfortable. Close your eyes.

As I count to 10, try to expose yourself more and more to the flashbacks or anxious images that you have been experiencing. If you haven't been experiencing any and are meditating so you can train your mind, try to think about the recent discomfort you have had regarding past flashbacks. Do not only notice the memory – try to really get into that situation. What were you wearing that day? Think about the weather. The smells. The sounds. Try to find some distinctive details that can help you transport yourself back to that particular moment in the past. It may be painful or scary or extremely anxious to do so. But remind yourself that you are doing this so you can overcome these images and learn how to stop them from interfering with your life. Now, transport yourself back in time.

1, 2, 3, 4, 5, 6, 7, 8, 9, 10.

You may be frightened or under a lot of stress at the moment, but that's okay. Let yourself feel whatever it is that you are feeling. Flashbacks and anxious images from the past live only in your head. They belong to an inner world you have created for yourself. The only way you can let go of these anxieties and stop replaying these images is if you get out of your head and focus on the outer world instead.

Your flashbacks are not real. They are not facts. They are not happening in the present. You are safe. Nothing can hurt or make you feel sad at this moment. Whatever has been causing you pain and discomfort is not an actual thing from the present. It is something that has been over for quite some time now. It is only in your head. So let's escape your inner world, shall we?

Before you distract yourself, let's first knock down some of that tension by focusing on the breath for a couple of minutes.

Start breathing, deeply, and slowly, and repeat in your mind: *These images are not real. These images do not happen in the present.*

Inhale—2, 3. Exhale slowly.

Breathe in. These images are not real. Breathe out slowly.

Inhale—2, 3. Exhale.

Breathe in. These images do not happen in the present. Breathe out.

Breathe in.

Breathe out.

Breathe in.

Breathe out.

The best way to rid of the flashbacks is to focus on something that is happening at the moment, in the outer world; something that you are surrounded with. But that does not mean that you cannot minimize the significance of these flashbacks within your inner world. Regardless of what your flashback or anxious image is about, one thing is sure – it comes from the past. So, let's try something together.

When your mind gets visited by these ghosts from the pasts, try to focus all of your attention on something positive that happened to you during that time. It doesn't matter how far in the past the flashback belongs, try to find something good about that time. Think of a time when you were satisfied, a happy memory, a special occasion. Something positive that you can draw your attention to. Let your mind get transported back in time. Enjoy this moment. Include all your senses and try to really feel what it was like going through that moment. The sights, the smell. Make sure to capture it well, and stay there for a minute or two. Stay there and breathe.

Breathe in. Relax. Breathe out.

Breathe in. You are okay. Breathe out.

Breathe in. You are content. Breathe out.

Inhale. 2. 3. Exhale.

Inhale. 2. 3. Exhale.

Stay in this moment and focus on the positive feelings that you were experiencing back then. Try to feel just as content, pleased, relaxed. If the anxious images find their way back in, that's okay. Before you let them take over and fill you with distress, try to distract yourself with the outer world, the present.

Start by rubbing your fingers together. Focus all your energy there. Imagine that your whole body is involved in this simple friction. Feel the tickling sensation as you slowly rub the fingers together. Now, increase the pace. Rub faster and faster. Feel the skin on your fingers getting warmer and warmer. Focus on that. That is the present. That is what's really happening in this very moment. The images in your head are not real. They are not here.

Now, pinch both of your thighs gently, and stay in this position. Make sure to be gentle – you just need to apply some pressure, enough to feel it. You don't want to bruise yourself. Feel the tension in your thighs, and focus all of your attention there. Can you notice how, when all of your energy is drawn there, it almost feels as if the pressure is growing stronger and stronger? That is what's happening at this moment. That is what you are going through. The images in your head are not real.

Release the pressure, and place your hands back at your sides, or whatever their initial position was. Now that you are feeling present and relaxed, take a deep breath. Keep breathing deeply and calmly.

Breathe in.

Breathe out.

Breathe in.

Breathe out.

If you need more time and are unable to relax just yet, it is okay to do another return-to-present exercise. Squeeze your arm, tap your knees, or wiggle your toes for a minute or two. The point is to do something that will give your body a physical nudge to send a signal to your brain and let it know – you are here. You are in the present. The images in your head are not. Then breathe in. And breathe out.

Breathe in.

Breathe out.

Keep breathing until you can feel a deep relaxation take over.

If your equilibrium gets distracted by a flashback again, it is okay. It is time to face these anxious images and let them go once and for all. When a specific flashback pops up into your head, do not ignore it. Instead, try to face it.

Imagine separating yourself from the image. Instead of you playing a part of it, imagine that you are just an observer. Now, imagine that you are moving further and further away from it, but you are still watching. As you are moving away, the image gets smaller and smaller. Right now, the flashback is a mere image on a screen. And you, sitting in front of the screen, feel like you are watching a movie; not a scene from your actual past life. Do your best to get the full experience – picture, sound, real feelings. Allow yourself to experience the moment all over again, emotionally involved, but do not get personal. Remember, you are just watching a movie. It may be frightening at first, but try to detach yourself from the situation. You are not a star in the movie. You are merely an observer. This is not happening to you know. You are just replaying things. You have everything on a screen in front of you.

Now, imagine yourself holding a remote. You can actually choose whether you want to watch the flashback or not. Imagine hitting 'pause'. The image freezes. See? The image is not real. These anxious feelings cannot hurt you now. They are not happening in real life. As you realize that these flashbacks do not have any power over you, you feel a sense of tranquility build up.

You are safe.

You are here and now.

Inhale.

Exhale.

Breathe in.

Breathe out.

Now, turn the screen off, and watch the image disappear from the screen. You are no longer observing your flashbacks. All you can see now is nothing. Everything is blank.

You are safe.

You are here and now.

Your images and flashbacks are not real. They shouldn't have any control over your life.

Breathe in.

Breathe out.

As I count to 20, you will fall deeper and deeper into a state of complete serenity. You relieve yourself from these images. You allow yourself to relax and be calm.

1, 2, 3, 4, 5, 6, 7, 8, 9, 10, 11, 12, 13, 14, 15, 16, 17, 18, 19, 20.

Slowly, open your eyes. Take some time to become aware of your surroundings. Look around the room, notice the smell, sound, be present.

You can use this meditation practice to train yourself to distract yourself with physical nudges you will give to your body. Next time an unwanted flashback appears, rub your fingers or pinch your arm and try to focus your attention on the physical state of that are of your body instead. Also, practice looking at your anxious images as watching a movie, and practice detachment from unwanted situations or memories.

With each practice, you will get better and better, and each time you manage to win the battle against your flashbacks, you are one step closer to winning the war. In the end, they will be nothing more than dots of old memories that you will not be even able to recognize.

Guided Meditation for Overcoming Depression and Knocking Down Intense Feelings of Anxiety (30 minutes)

Duration: 30 minutes

Welcome to this guided meditation for overcoming symptoms of depression, knocking down intense anxiety, and training your body and mind to relax and stay calm. For 30 minutes, you will join me on a relaxing journey of visualization that will help you let go of the dark cloud that has been overshadowing you and bring clarity to your mind.

Through this practice, you will not only be able to create a safe escape where you can go and relax wherever you feel the tension piling up, but you can also gain a better understanding of your overall well-being.

For starters, let's find a quiet place where you can relax and be undisturbed for approximately half an hour. Settle into a comfortable position – whether sitting or lying down – and close your eyes. Before we begin, prepare yourself mentally for deep relaxation.

Let's start this practice by counting to 20. As I slowly say the numbers, you imagine yourself slowly detaching from your surrounding and entering a new world. A safe place where we will leave all the darkness behind and learn to embrace calmness and serenity.

Take a deep breath, and let's go.

1, 2, 3. Keep breathing slowly.

6, 7, 8. Inhale and exhale.

10, 11, 12. Leaving the negativity behind.

15, 16, 17. Almost there.

19, 20.

Imagine yourself being found in a strange and empty place. A place that has no walls, no doors, no ceiling. It seems as though you are sitting in a never-ending universe of emptiness. You look around, trying to see something at least, but there is really nothing. No sound, nothing. A complete blankness. It seems frightening at first, but as you stand there, in the middle of nowhere, you see that it is quite calming and relieving.

The only thing that you can notice is the marble floor. It is white, shiny, and cold. You sit down, barefoot, allowing the coolness of the stone to touch your feet, the only sensation you can feel in this place. Stay in that position, placing your focus on how your feet feel. As you are directing all of your energy in your feet, it seems as though the rest of your body is becoming numb. Your whole body sleeps. Only your feet are alive, only there you can feel something. How does that feel?

You finally get accustomed to the coolness of the marble. It is starting to grow on you. It feels good. It feels familiar. But, all of a sudden, you feel your whole body, feet included, getting warmer and warmer. You look ahead, and you see a ray of sunshine, illuminating a path ahead of you.

You stand up, slowly, and start walking toward the light. As you get closer, you realize that the pathway is actually made of clouds. You are walking on clouds. Only these clouds are not just air. They are soft, cottony, pillow-like clouds. You are still barefoot. Each step you take, you feel your feet gently pressing against the cushiony texture. Your feet feel comfortable. You feel the softness against your skin, and it makes you feel good. Focus on that feeling. Try to imagine what walking on such soft texture really feels like. Draw all of your energy to your feet. The sponginess underneath uplifts your mood instantly. It relaxes your whole body. It feels like you can walk this pathway for hours without getting tired.

Keep walking.

You are alone. There is nobody around. You do not need to pretend or put on a good mood for someone else's sake. Just keep walking this path and try to relax. Allow yourself to be the real you. See how it feels to be in your skin when you are all alone. When there are no expectations. When you have no obligations, no worries from the outer world.

Keep walking the path.

With each step you take, you feel lighter and lighter. It is almost like the clouds absorb your weight. You are walking so effortlessly, that it almost feels like you are barely even touching the clouds. It is almost like you are floating. Allow your whole body to feel this sensation.

You are walking.

And walking.

You are alone. It feels good to be free of the things that make you feel entrapped in the world. It feels good to get to be yourself. Enjoy being in your own skin. Often, depression symptoms involve a feeling of worthlessness. But, as you are walking this soft path, a reassuring feeling takes over, and you are feeling more comfortable in your skin.

Keep walking and focus on this feeling. You are worthy. You are strong. You are free. Relax your mind, get rid of tension. Just focus on this feeling of worthiness. Focus on the softness of your steps, as well. Keep walking and free your mind.

If anxiety finds its way back again, think of it as a black cloud that overshadows you and your path. The path of clouds is illuminated by the sun, but now, with your anxiety and negative feelings present, there is a giant black cloud overhead, casting a vast shadow over you and the soft clouds you are walking on. You cannot escape it. It follows you with every step, affecting your mood, disrupting your relaxed state of mind. Do not let it guide its way. You may have been feeling depressed or severely anxious for a long time, but that does not mean that you cannot choose to snap out of that negativity. It is all in you. You have the power to escape. Repeat this in your mind with me.

I have the power to escape.

I have the power to escape.

I have the power to escape.

Do not get into your negative thoughts at this point. They are nothing. They have no meaning to you. If you give them the attention and the power to guide you, they will start spreading all over your mind, tainting your thoughts, polluting your emotions, dragging you to darkness. If you give them the attention at this point, the black cloud overhead will spread and spread until it swallows you completely. Instead, repeat it in your mind with me:

I have the power to escape.

I have the power to escape.

I have the power to escape.

Bring your attention to your feet and the way it feels to be pressing against the softness of these cottony clouds. But this time, try to increase the pace. Start walking a little faster, and faster, as if you are trying to run away from the cloud overhead. As you are speed walking, you see the dark cloud become smaller and smaller. As it decreases in size, the path becomes illuminated once again. Keep speeding ahead. You can escape from your negativity. You choose not to be affected by it.

You put all of your focus on the way your feet press onto the comfortable texture. On the sensation of the sun warming your skin. Soft and warm, you are slowly starting to relax. You let go off your negativity. You choose to be free. You look up, but there is nothing but a black speck that is slowly fading away. You take another step, and the darkness is gone. You are free once again.

Decrease your pace. Walk slowly and refocus your energy and attention on the softness of the pillow-like path and how this comfortable texture feels on the skin at the bottom of your feet. It is warm, light, and you are safe.

Keep focusing on this comfortable feeling. And as I count to 20, you are falling into deep relaxation.

1, 2, 3, 4, 5, 6, 7, 8, 9, 10, 11, 12, 13, 14, 15, 16, 17, 18, 19, 20.

You are relaxed now. You have made it to the end of the path. Imagine sitting down and crossing your legs. It almost feels as if you have settled into the clouds' lap, the softness holding you comfortably, the pillow-like texture reassuring on your skin. You look ahead, and you see a rainbow. It is bright and vivid. Too vivid to be true even. And it is so close. Imagine yourself reaching with your hand and touching it. It is made of air, but as you move your fingers through it, you see the colors dance around your hand. The red, the orange, yellow, green, the blue colors, violet… As I count to 10, you will stay in this moment, imagining yourself sitting on the clouds, watching the colors of the rainbows float in the air in front of you. Focus on how relaxing and liberating it is to be by yourself, in your safe, private universe. Free from your thoughts, free from worries. Simply enjoying being in your own skin.

1, 2, 3, 4, 5, 6, 7, 8, 9, 10.

If your equilibrium gets interrupted by an anxious feeling or negative emotion that intensifies the symptoms of depression, just take a deep breath and exhale slowly. As the breath goes out, imagine that your negativity also leaves your body.

Inhale. Exhale.

Imagine the negativity to be a black smoke that comes out of your nostrils and getting lost behind the colorful rainbow.

You do not allow the negativity to affect you. You choose to let it go. Focus on the colors of the rainbows again. Vivid and cheerful, they bring an uplifting sensation to your body and mind. You are relaxed.

Take a deep breath. Echale slowly.

Breathe in.

Breathe out.

Breathe in.

Breathe out.

Slowly, open your eyes now. Look around you and notice your surroundings. You may be drawn back to the real world, but there is no need for you to carry all that negative weight on your shoulders. Whenever you feel yourself being dragged back to that vicious cycle of unwanted thoughts and emotions, just return back to the path of clouds, start walking toward the rainbow, and try to relax. You can choose to be free of the negativity. You can escape the anxiety and feel good in your own skin. You can enjoy your life, relaxed and comfortable.

Sense-Focusing Meditation for Stopping Unwanted Thoughts and Overcoming Anxious and Stressful Feelings (30 minutes)

Duration: 30 minutes

Sometimes, when we cannot hush our busy minds or when our daily chores get interrupted by negative thoughts and feelings that take our focus and energy away from the things that matter, we just need to distract ourselves, to regain a deep understanding of what is going on around us at that time.

This 30-minute meditation practice will help you put every shred of energy within you on your senses. Through your sense of sight, smell, touch, taste, and hearing, you will train your mind to slowly back away from the negativity, and shift the focus to the present moment. This great mindfulness technique is the perfect tool for putting a stop to overthinking, as well as decreasing anxiety and stress.

To begin, make sure that you find a comfortable place where you can settle and not be disrupted for approximately 30 minutes. Also, make sure that your phone and other devices are turned off. This place can be either a corner in your room, your backyard, the nearest park – wherever you can relax. Sit comfortably. If you can – and are comfortable with – cross your legs. If not, find a sitting position that will help you relax. Do not close your eyes for this practice – lower the eyelids a bit if you cannot relax with your eyes wide open, but do not close them completely.

Let's begin by relaxing ourselves first. You need to be relaxed and then disturbed by an unpleasant sensation or thought to learn how to distract yourself and draw your attention elsewhere.

I will count to ten, and as I do so, you will start focusing on your breath.

1, 2, 3, 4, 5, 6, 7, 8, 9, 10.

Take a deep breath. Hold it. 2, 3. Exhale slowly.

Inhale slowly and deeply. 1, 2, 3. Breathe out through your nose.

Notice how your lungs widen when you inhale and how they shrink when the breath leaves your body.

Inhale.

Exhale.

Inhale.

Exhale.

You are feeling more and more relaxed with each breath you take. It feels good to be this comfortable. An uplifting sensation runs through your body, telling you that it is good to be alive. It is good to be right here at this moment. The more you breathe, the more you enjoy this feeling.

Breathe in.

Breathe out.

Deeply. Slowly.

Breathe in. Hold it. 2, 3. Exhale.

Inhale deeply. 1, 2, 3. Breathe out through your nose.

Now that you are feeling relaxed let yourself just be in this moment. Try not to think of anything else, just keep your attention to your breath.

When a thought or emotion pops up and shatters your tranquility, we will distract ourselves then. For now, just focus on your breath. If you are still feeling relaxed, you can pause this script and just allow yourself to enjoy yourself.

Once distracted, try not to overthink the thought or emotion. Just, acknowledge its presence, and shift your attention to your senses. Let's start with your eyes. They are already open or half-open so that you can see your surroundings. Try to focus on the things you can see. Again, do not get into details, just observe, and acknowledge.

If you are in your room, look around and see familiar objects, pictures, maybe clothing items. You feel secure looking at them; they provide you a sense of safety. Reassurance that you are within your comfort zone.

If you are outside, notice your surroundings. Look up and see the sky, the clouds, the sun. Flowers, trees, birds, people passing by in the distance perhaps. Acknowledge whatever's going on around you without giving these objects of observation any more attention than that. We are only trying to distract ourselves.

Look down and notice the surface you are sitting on. Is it a carpet, a wooden floor, a mat, grass? Slowly move your eyes upward, focusing your gaze in front of you. Stay in this position.

Now, let's move our attention from our eyes to our ears. Focus on what you can hear. If you are outside, there surely are different sounds that you can focus yourself on. The chirping of the birds, the buzzing of the bees, you can maybe hear crickets. Is it windy? Focus on the sound that wind makes when it gets tangled between tree branches and leaves. Are there people nearby? Focus on the distant chatter.

If you are indoors and are not alone at home, focus on the sound your family members make in the other room. Keep your attention there for a while. If there is no sound you can make, that is perfectly fine. We will just focus on the silence instead. Stay in this moment, hearing whatever sound there is, and just relax.

If an emotion overpowers or a thought creeps in, that is okay. The important thing is not to engage in these feelings and emotions, but gently move your attention to the present. Something that is happening here and now. Something that is real at this moment.

Gently, without judging, move your attention to the smell that is in the air. Indoors, you can maybe focus on a room freshener, the scent of your perfume, hand cream, fabric softener. Perhaps you have a scented candle lit. Focus on that.

If you are outdoors, focus on the way the grass smells, the scent of the flowers. Perhaps the ground is moist. Focus on the earthiness of that scent. Just keep your attention there and merely acknowledge it.

Slowly, shift your focus from your nose to your mouth. Let's focus on the taste. What kind of taste is that? Is it sweet? Sour? Perhaps you've recently taken a chewing gum. Focus on the minty taste. Or maybe you've had candy, and there is a pleasant sweet taste in your mouth now. If you are having trouble focusing on the taste in your mouth and you cannot really distinguish it, try licking your lips. Our lips are not affected by saliva so there are high chances that your taste buds can detect something. Focus on that.

It is okay to get distracted. Do not beat yourself over it. You are only human. Instead of reasoning why you are feeling these emotions or having such thoughts, try to detach your focus from them, by placing your attention back to your senses.

This time, let's focus on your sense of touch and your skin, in general. Start by placing your hand on your legs, touching the material of your clothes.

How does that feel? Is it soft? Smooth? Is the surface maybe uneven? Run your fingers over the material and see how that feels.

If there is a breeze, let yourself really feel it. Allow it to go through your hair, tickle your skin, bring a note of coolness to your face. Take a moment to enjoy this. If you are outside on the sun, feel it warming your skin, wrapping its rays over it like a comfort blanket, providing safety.

Now, focus on the clothes you are wearing. How do they feel on your skin? Are they comfortable and loose? Do they keep you warm? Do they allow the breeze to cool you down?

Now go down to your feet. If you are barefoot, feel the surface you are sitting on. Is it smooth, uneven? Warm, cold? Is the grass tickling your toes? Focus yourself on the sensations that run all over your skin.

When you get disrupted by a thought or emotion, gently bring the attention back to your skin, nose, mouth, ears, or eyes. Do not allow yourself to slip into the darkness. Instead, stay in the present, aware and observing. Focus on the things that are surrounding you, not the destructive thoughts that occupy your mind. Relax your whole being by choosing to step away from these emotions, and draw your energy back to your senses. The senses are real. That is how you really feel at this moment. Comfortable and calm.

Let's finish this practice by taking the relaxation to a deeper level. By focusing on our breath, we will fall into a deep state of calmness and peacefulness. A place where anxiety and negative thoughts are not allowed. Someplace when only you and air exist.

Take a deep breath. Hold it. 2, 3. Exhale.

Take another breath. 1, 2, 3. Exhale.

Breathe in deeply.

Breathe out slowly.

Breathe in.

Breathe out.

Slowly inhale.

And exhale.

Take another breath.

And release it gently.

Inhale.

Exhale.

As I count to 10, you will gently bring your awareness back to your surroundings.

1, 2, 3, 4, 5, 6, 7, 8, 9, 10.

Now that your eyes are fully open, you can gently stretch your body, allowing the blood flow to run through your legs, reach your toes. Look around you and absorb all that it is happening. Include all of your senses now, to see, smell, taste, touch, and hear the environment.

This sense-focused meditation is an excellent tool for being aware, stopping your mind from overthinking, releasing tension and anxiety, and improve concentration and focus. Make sure to practice it regularly, but also, try to involve your senses more in the real world, so you can train your mind and teach yourself how to keep your focus on the things that matter to you at a particular moment.

Meditation for Surpassing Pressure-Fueled Anxieties (30 minutes)

Duration: 30 minutes

More often than not, people feel intense feelings of anxiety whenever they find themselves in a high-pressure environment. It seems as though it is impossible to calm yourself down right before a job interview, an important public appearance, or whatever it is that puts you under pressure and causes anxiety to cloud your mind.

This 30-minute meditation will not only help you relax right before such a big moment, but you can also use this practice to train your mind to snap out of these pressure-fueled anxieties gradually. With these skills of relaxation and calming down that you will learn through this practice, you can learn how to better cope with such situations and remain calm and comfortable in your own skin.

This meditation practice uses breathing, muscle relaxation, visualization, and calming the thoughts as a way to relieve pressure anxiety.

Now, sit comfortably, get rid of distractions, and close your eyes.

First, let's concentrate on your breath. The way you breathe plays a crucial part in how relaxed or tense you will be in certain situations, so learning to do it slowly and gently when faced with pressure is of great significance.

Take a deep breath through your nose. Hold it. Now, release it slowly, through the nose.

Breathe in deeply. Breathe out slowly.

Breathe in. Breathe out.

Breathe in. Breathe out.

Calm yourself by focusing your energy on your breath. Feel it through your nose, in your lungs, your chest puff up. Now exhale slowly. Notice how your chest come down, feel the breath leave your nostrils. It may help you relax even better if you count while breathing deeply.

Breathe in deeply. 1, 2, 3. Breatthe out.

Inhale and hold the breath. 1, 2, 3. Breathe out.

Inhale. 1, 2, 3. Breathe out.

Now, let's try to breathe in and out for three seconds.

Breathe in – 1, 2, 3. Breathe out – 1, 2, 3.

Inhale deeply. Hold it, 2, 3. Exhale – 1, 2, 3.

Breathe in – 1, 2, 3. Breathe out – 1, 2, 3.

Deeply in – 1, 2, 3. Slowly out – 1, 2, 3.

Now, I will count to ten. With each number, you are getting more and more relaxed, focusing on the way you breathe.

1, 2, 3, 4, 5, 6, 7, 8, 9, 10.

Now that you are more relaxed, let's try focusing on your muscles. We do not want our attention in the biceps or the abdominal area, but the muscles that are the most affected when you find yourself tense and under a lot of pressure. Those include the muscles in your jaw, shoulders, and hands. When faced with a high-pressure situation, our jaw and hands are usually clenched, and our shoulders are tense. But, for you to be able to relax those muscles, you first need to expose them to some tension.

The breathing practice relaxed your body and mind, but now, it is time to put it back into pressure mode so you can learn how to relax the affected muscles in those situations. So, before we learn to do that, let's imagine you are in an intense-pressure environment.

Think about the particular situation that has been causing you distress. Think about what you have to do in this situation. Imagine your heartbeat getting faster and faster. You are there now. It is happening. Why does this put that much pressure on you? Focus on the thoughts that arise at this moment. Focus on the feelings of unease, the anxiety swooping in. You feel the nervousness rising. The suspense causes you in distress. Your shoulders are tense, your jaw is getting tight, the hands are clenched.

Now, try to shift your attention from the pressure situation to the body areas that are clearly under a lot of pressure. Let's start with the shoulders. How do they feel? Feel the tension that is there; the tightness that keeps them in distress. Once you can really feel the pressure, start lowering the shoulders. Do this slowly and consciously. Feel them become softer and softer. As they are loosening, you are getting more relaxed.

When you soften the shoulder area, shift your attention to your jaw. Notice the tightness that is there. Slowly, start loosening. Let go of the tension that is there gently, and make sure that your teeth are not touching. You are letting go of the pressure. Let your jaw and mouth soften.

Now, shift to your hands. How do they feel? Gently and slowly, open your hands, and let your arms fall at your sides, loosely. You are getting more and more relaxed.

If you are still feeling tense, then perhaps there is a great deal of tension piled up elsewhere. Scan your body now and check which area is under pressure. Starting at your feet, gently move your attention upwards, toward your head, scanning each body part for tension. When you find an area that needs softening, make sure to loosen it. Do this for as long as it takes for your body to be relaxed and free of tightness.

Your body may be relaxed, but you still have to work into putting your mind into a deep state of relaxation to avoid being dragged back to unease, shortly. Now, let's bring the attention back to your breath. Take a deep breath through your nose, and feel the air make your chase rise and puff up. Breathe out through your nose, and acknowledge the breath going out of your nostrils.

Breathe in.

Breathe out.

Breathe in.

Breathe out.

Take a deep breath. Feel it leave your body through your nose.

Deeply in. Slowly out.

Breathe in.

Breathe out.

As I count to 10, you are getting more and more relaxed. With each breath you take, you fall deeper into a world of total calmness.

1, 2, 3, 4, 5, 6, 7, 8, 9, 10.

You are calm.

You are relaxed.

Stay in this moment and just focus on your breath.

If you feel the tension rising and you find your mind affected by pressure-fueled anxiety again, it may be so because your situation is of considerable significance to you. To let go of the tension, you may have to convince yourself that you choose not to be affected by it.

When feelings of distress regarding a pressure situation revisit you, try to engage. Again, like in the beginning of this practice, try to pinpoint the source of pressure. What causes you to feel this way? What are you most anxious about? Get into it and acknowledge where the distress is coming from. When you realize what causes you to feel this way, it is time to address it.

Breathing calmly, imagine yourself in this exact situation. But, this time, instead of focusing on the things that bring you anxiety and make your jaw and hands clench, imagine a different scenario. This time, imagine yourself thriving under pressure. That's right. You are getting on top of the situation, finding a solution, fixing whatever's there to be fixed. You are no longer afraid because there is nothing to be afraid of.

You can beat this.

You are strong to beat this.

You are no longer afraid of the pressure.

The pressure makes you strong.

It is there to motivate you and push you to succeed.

Take a deep breath to the count of three – 1, 2, 3. Hold it. 1, 2. Exhale slowly. 1, 2, 3.

Keep breathing deeply and slowly, imagining yourself thriving.

If it is a job interview, imagine yourself getting the best job possible under great conditions. If it is a public speech that makes you tense, envision yourself knocking everyone's socks off. Whatever it is, imagine the best possible scenario. Now, try to really believe it. Think about what this turn of events brings. Try to get into more details. A better job means a better car, vacationing abroad… Or maybe your scenario brings you recognition, respect, a show of gratitude... Imagine your preferred outcome, but do not just acknowledge – try to actually visualize. See yourself out there, prospering, flourishing. Get into these emotions. How does it feel to thrive?

Continue breathing and let these feel-good vibes fill your whole being, relaxing your body, bringing ease to your mind.

Breathe in.

Breathe out.

Breathe in.

Breathe out.

As I count to 10, you get more and more convinced that you can really excel. Focus on the numbers, continue breathing calmly, and imagine yourself performing rather exceptional.

1, 2, 3, 4, 5, 6, 7, 8, 9, 10.

Now, take a deep breath to the count of three, and as you do so, open your eyes gently.

1, 2, 3.

Exhale slowly through your nose.

Notice your surroundings, stretch, keep your body relaxed, and try to preserve that feeling of comfort you've experienced during this practice. Whatever you find yourself in a high-pressure environment, focus on relaxing the affected muscles first, and then try to visualize yourself excelling. Training your mind to do so will help you better cope with pressure and relieve yourself from intense feelings of anxiety.

Guided Meditation for Letting Go of Unwanted Thoughts (20 minutes)

Duration: 20 minutes

Welcome to this guided meditation that will take you on a relaxing journey of letting go. With this 20-minute meditation practice, you will be able to get rid of the thoughts that disrupt your calm state of mind and detach yourself from negativity. With the power of visualization, imagination, and your will to be positive and truly content, I will guide you to a safe place where you will feel completely tranquil.

For starters, find a comfortable place and settle in a position that will not bring you discomfort in the next 20 minutes. You can either be sitting or lying down. As long as you are comfortable, it doesn't matter. Close your eyes and take one deep breath.

Exhale.

Inhale deeply – exhale slowly.

Deeply in – slowly out.

As I count to 20, you will continue breathing slowly and calmly, focusing on the numbers, imagining yourself falling deeper and deeper into a dark pit. Try to really feel what it is like to be falling down.

1, 2, 3 - you are falling down.

6, 7, 8 – deeper and deeper.

11, 12, 13, 14 – we're almost there

17, 18, 19, 20.

We have stopped falling. You are now sitting down a cold surface. It is still dark. Pitch black. You cannot see anything. You are alone. Sit there for a few moments, allowing your thoughts to take over your mind. Worries, uncertainties, anxieties. Let them all in. Do not engage with the thoughts or feelings individually, but allow yourself to feel the intensity of their presence. Acknowledge that they are there. They are real, and they clearly affect you.

I will slowly count to 5, and you will be focused on that distress and unease.

1, 2, 3, 4, 5.

Now that you know how much these images or sensations bother you, it is time for you to detach yourself from them. Only by choosing to separate your being from your thoughts and emotions can you be able to control what is felt and what is worth thinking over.

Let's do it slowly and gently. To start, let's draw all of the negativity out of your body. Imagine your thoughts, emotions, images, anxious sensations, or whatever it is that has been polluting your mind, as a smoke. A dark energy that is dancing inside your head, making you worry, be anxious, and unable to relax. Now, focus on that energy. Envision the smoke floating inside your head, acknowledging its presence. Slowly, start dragging the smoke downward, purging it out of your body.

Imagine a strong, outer force dragging that dark energy down your face, through the neck, abdomen, legs. You can feel the negativity being forced out. It has lowered to your feet now, making them heavy. Try to feel that sensation. Your feet feel as if they are about to explode. But the only thing that explodes is that dark energy. It leaves your body, and you can actually see it underneath your feet. You can stomp it, feel it. It is thick, heavy, dark. Those are the thoughts you don't want to engage with. The emotions that you do not want to feel.

Keep it underneath your feet and repeat in your mind: I am free from negativity. I am free from negativity. I am starting to relax. I am no longer anxious.

Take a deep breath. Hold it, one, two. Exhale.

Inhale.

Exhale.

I am free from unwanted thoughts.

I am free from anxiety.

You are stomping over the smoke. You are letting go of distress.

Breathe in.

Breathe out.

Breathe in.

Breathe out.

You are slowly starting to relax. You can feel the tension decreasing, your muscles loosening. It feels good to be free of those thoughts.

Now, imagine your body starting to float over the darkness of thoughts. The energy is no longer underneath your feet. You are slowly moving upwards, leaving the dark energy at the bottom of the pit.

There is a force pushing your body upwards, making you fly back to where you came from. As you are flying over the darkness, you realize that you are lighter now. The heavy thoughts and emotions are no longer present in your mind. There is no negativity to weigh you down this time. You almost feel like a feather in the air.

You are safe.

You are relaxed.

You are flying back to safety, leaving the darkness behind you.

You choose to be calm.

Breathe calmly, focusing on the sensation of being light in the air. Of moving upwards as a rocket, but slowly and comfortably.

As I count to 20, you will stay focused on this sensation, trying to imagine what flying lightly really feels like. Slowly, almost like floating. Feeling the light air tickling your skin.

1, 2 3, 4, 5, 6, 7, 8, 9, 10, 11, 12, 13, 14, 15, 16, 17, 18, 19, 20.

You look up now and see that the source of light is getting bigger and bigger. You are slowly moving toward the place you came from. You are returning back, but without any worries to keep you down. You've left them all down in the hole. You can almost feel the sun warming your skin, illuminating your face. You are getting closer and closer. Finally, you arrive. You are no longer flying. You look back to see that the hole is getting closed. You are watching patiently, waiting for your negative thoughts and emotions to be closed forever.

1, 2, 3, 4, 5. The hole is no longer there. You have buried your worries and can finally relax.

Breathing slowly, you feel your whole being entering a deep state of relaxation. You weel different now. Calm. Safe. Happy.

As I count to 5, you will slowly open your eyes and bring your awareness to your surroundings.

1, 2, 3, 4, 5.

You are here and now, present. You are relaxed and comfortable. You can go back to your daily activities knowing that you've managed to escape the negativity.

Wherever you feel like your thoughts or emotions are getting too intense, just fall back into the pit, burying them, relaxing your entire being.

Guided Meditation for Deep Relaxation (20 minutes)

Duration: 20 minutes

This guided meditation uses a sense of falling at the beginning of the practice. If you've done the previous one, then you may be familiar with how this sense of falling can be used to let go of your unwanted thoughts and emotions. But here, we will not focus on leaving the negativity behind. This 20-minute meditation will guide you into a peaceful place, focusing on bringing your entire being into a deep state of calmness and tranquility.

This can be practiced after a long and hectic day, to soothe your mind and body, or it can be just as beneficial in the morning if you wish to start your day with calmness and positive energy.

Let's begin. Start by finding a place where you will be able to settle comfortably and stay uninterrupted for approximately 20 minutes. You can either sit down and cross your legs or lay flat on your back with your hands behind your head.

As I slowly count to 20, you will start detaching your being from the reality. You will let go of any thoughts and emotions that you may be experiencing at the moment. You will just focus on your breath, breathing slowly and calmly. As the numbers increase, you will become more detached and more ready to relax.

Take a deep breath now, and release it slowly out of your nose.

A breath in. A breath out.

Inhale. Exhale.

Now, you are getting detached and free from any feelings and thoughts. Focus on the numbers, and keep breathing.

1, 2, 3, 4, 5, 6, 7, 8, 9, 10, 11, 12, 13, 14, 15, 16, 17, 18, 19, 20.

As you are getting away from real sensations, imagine you are floating in the sky. The air is light; there is no pressure. You are feeling comfortable and free. You look down, and you see a forest. Its thickness does not allow you to peek inside; all you can see are the tips of the trees, the top branches and upper leaves. They are green, illuminated by the sun that is also shining upon you at the moment. Your skin is getting warmer and you are enjoying the view. But it's not enough. You want to get a glimpse of the full picture. So you decide to go down, deep into the forest.

So you gently push your body down, applying mild pressure, just enough for you to steer and change the direction. Your hands and legs are in the air, feeling light, almost as they aren't even there. You are with your stomach down, focusing your gaze on the trees. You start falling, but you are moving so slow that you can notice every branch, see every crack. The trees are very tall, but you are going down at such slow pace that it feels as though you will never reach the ground. They keep stretching and stretching down, and you are still falling.

1, 2, 3 - still falling.

6, 7, 8 – you feel light and free.

11, 12, 13 – you notice the rays of sun intertwining and illuminating the trees' trunks.

18, 19, 20 – you are nearly there.

You are slowly landing. It feels good to be on your feet, but you still feel light and comfortable. There is nothing that is weighing you down.

Everything around you is green, vivid, and alive. You find a spot illuminated by the sun that has pierced through the branches, and you decide to settle there. Imagine yourself in the same position you are right now. If you are sitting with your legs crossed, imagine you taking the same position in the forest. If you are lying down, imagine doing just that. In either way, make sure that your head is illuminated by the sun. Your eyes are closed, and you tilt your head back slightly, allowing the rays to warm your face, gently caressing your skin.

Sit there and enjoy being free, alone, just you and this fantastic nature. Take a deep breath and focus on the scents in the air. The earthy notes of the ground you are sitting on, the smell of fresh grass, the fruits of the trees, the flowery tones of the scent that is dancing around your nose, tempting you to get up and explore the kinds of flowers that grow in this place.

Continue breathing calmly, and focus on the sounds. The relaxing buzzing of insects, the beautiful sound that the birds chirping makes. Imagine opening your eyes now, and seeing a little blue bird standing in front of you. It is looking you directly in the eyes as if it is waiting for you to reach with your hand. You open your palm and, without hesitation, it lands onto it, rewarding you with a melody that melts your heart. When it finally flies away, you watch it disappear in front of you until it becomes a blue speck in the distance. You close your eyes again, glad to be alive, happy to be able to breathe in such life, grateful that you are free and relaxed at this moment.

This forest, the brightness and warmth that the sun brings to your face, the sounds, the scents, they all become your own little paradise. A place where you can fall into wherever you need to let go and wind down. You are appreciative of this opportunity. You will no longer let your busy lifestyle wear you down and exhaust you. Why would you when you can be here, now, enjoying this view, absorbing this feel-good energy?

You take a deep breath, and as it fills your lungs and makes your chest puff up, you notice that you are being lifted up. As you are floating upwards,you get a chance to explore the trees again. The uneven surface of their trunks, the range of colors hidden between their leaves and fruits, the crown… You are flying back to where you came from, but you are different now. You are more relaxed, calmer, and bursting with positivity.

As I count to 10, you will become more and more soothed.

1, 2, 3, 4, 5, 6, 7, 8, 9, 10.

Now, open your eyes, and take in your surroundings. You are comfortable, calm, and at ease.

Breathing Meditation for Anxiety, Depression, and Overthinking (15 minutes)

Breathing calmly and slowly is an essential part of every meditation practice, but now, we will take things to another level. Spicing up regular breathing with colors, we give this practice life, brightness, and vividness, that will make you feel even more relaxed and at peace.

This practice is great for dealing with immediate anxieties and negative symptoms as it is an excellent unwinding tool that will help you knock stressful feelings down and provide you with a sense of comfort and security.

Sit comfortably someplace where you will be uninterrupted for 15 minutes, and close your eyes.

For starters, let's loosen up a bit by simply slowing your breath and focusing on breathing calmly. As I count to 10, you will become more and more relaxed, inhaling deeply, exhaling slowly, focusing on the numbers.

1, 2, 3, 4, 5, 6, 7, 8, 9, 10.

Now, before we begin with the colorful breathing technique, let's take a moment to acknowledge the breath first.

Take a deep breath to the count of three. 1, 2, 3. Hold it, 2. 3. Exhale - 1, 2, 3.

Let's do it again, but focus on the sensation that breathing the air brings to you. How it feels in your nostrils when it is breathed in, how your chest rises and falls, how it feels to breathe out.

A dep breath in – 1, 2, 3.

Hold it, 2, 3.

Exhale – 1, 2, 3.

Inhale – 1, 2, 3.

Hold, 2, 3.

Slowly out – 1, 2, 3.

Now, let's try something else. For this relaxation practice, we will breathe in deeply through the nose, but exhale through our mouth. Give it a try.

Breathe in deepy through your nose. Hold for 1, 2. Exhale slowly through your mouth.

Inhale through your nose deeply. Hold the breath. Breathe out through the mouth very slowly and calmly.

Let's do it again. Take a deep breath and focus on the way that the breath feels in your nose, lungs. Now, open your mind gently, and slowly start breathing out. As the air is getting out of your body, imagine that you can actually see it. Imagine it coming out of your body in the form of red smoke.

Now, breathe calmly for a few moments, and take the time to notice the red smoke disappear in front of you.

Do it again, but this time, let's use a yellow color.

Breathe in deeply through your nose. Hold it, 2, 3, Out through the mouth as a yellow smoke. Focus on the color; on how it is becoming brighter and brighter, disappearing in the air.

Take another deep breath. Hold it inside for a moment. Release it through your mouth gently and slowly. Thick blue smoke is going out of your mouth, getting thinner in thinner in front of you until it evaporates completely.

A deep breath in. Hold, 2, 3. Open your mouth and release green smoke. Watch it disappear for a couple of seconds.

Then again. Inhale deeply. Hold the breath for a moment. Breathe out through the mouth very slowly and watch an orange smoke disappear into thin air.

A deep breath in. Hold, 2, 3. Release through your mouth slowly, in the form of a purple smoke.

When you can no longer see the purple color in front of you, take another deep breath. Hold it for a moment. Now, release in the form of pink smoke, disappearing in front of you.

Take a deep breath. Hold, 2, 3. Grey smoke goes out of your mouth as you exhale. Watch it disappear.

Another deep breath in. Hold it for a moment or two. Then slowly, exhale through the mouth. Imagine brown smoke coming out of it, painting the air in front of you, and then disappearing with no trace.

Now, let's take one final deep breath. Hold it, 2, 3. Open your mouth gently, and let the breath out. It is colorful, only this time, it is not a single color. The smoke that goes out of your mouth is made of all the colors from before. It is red, yellow, blue, green, orange, purple, pink, grey, brown. And instead of disappearing and evaporating, this time, the colors just sit in the air, floating around, painting the room with bright and vivid colors.

Spend some time watching them dance around in front of you. Breathe slowly and calmly, and enjoy the colorful view.

Breathe in.

Breathe out.

Breathe in.

Breathe out.

Breathe in.

Breathe out.

Inhale.

Exhale.

Now, I'm going to count to 10, and the colors in front of you will slowly start to fade away. With each number, they become more transparent and transparent.

1, 2, 3, 4, 5, 6, 7, 8, 9, 10.

Gently, open your eyes and bring your awareness to your surroundings. You are feeling relaxed and calm.

Meditation for Calming a Busy Mind (15 minutes)

Duration: 15 minutes

When you cannot put a stop to the whirlwind of thoughts in your head, and it seems as though you cannot hush your busy mind, you are in desperate need for an unwinding tool. Luckily this 15-minute meditation practice is just the thing you need to calm yourself down, stop the overthinking cycle, and just relax.

With the power of cue words and positive affirmations that you will repeat to yourself in your mind, you will be able to bring back order to your hectic mind.

Now, sit comfortably, close your eyes, and let's begin.

Let's start by focusing ourselves on the breath. Take a deep breath and feel it in your nostrils, slowly filling your lungs, making your chest rise. Hold it there for 1, 2, and release slowly, through the nostrils again, and out of your body.

Again, take a deep breath, hold it for a moment, then breathe out through your nose, focusing on how the air feels when leaving your body.

A deep breath in. Hold, 1, 2. Release slowly.

Breathe in deeply.

Wait a moment.

Breathe out slowly.

Breathe in.

Hold, 1, 2.

Breathe out slowly.

A deep inhale.

Wait, 1, 2.

Exhale slowly through your nose.

Inhale.

Hold, 1, 2.

Exhale.

When your focus gets interrupted and a thought distracts you, just continue breathing, but this time, repeat some cues. When you are taking a breath, say "I let you go" and when you exhale, say "Relax".

Breathe in – *I let you go*

Breathe out – *Relax*

Breathe in – *I let you go*

Breathe out – *Relax*

Inhale – *I let you go*

Breathe out – *Relax*

Now, I am going to count to 30, and you will continue breathing slowly and calmly, while repeating the same cue words in your mind. *I let you go. Relax.*

1, 2, 3, 4, 5, 6, 7, 8, 9, 10, 11, 12, 13, 14, 15, 16, 17, 18, 19, 20, 21, 22, 23, 24, 25, 26, 27, 28, 29, 30.

Continue brething some more.

I let you go.

Relax.

I let you go.

Relax.

I let you go.

Relax.

If you get distracted again, gently acknowledge those thoughts, but do not engage. Just repeat to yourself:

I am not my thoughts.

My thoughts aren't facts. They are not reality.

These images aren't real.

My thoughts do not affect me.

I am choosing to be free of them.

I am choosing to relax.

I am free.

I am comfortable.

I am falling deeper and deeper into a state of tranquility.

Now, breathe in again. *I let you go.* Breathe out - *Relax.*

Breathe in – I let you go.

Breathe out – Relax.

Inhale – I let you go.

Exhale slowly – Relax.

Keep breathing calmly, reminding yourself that you choose not to be affected by your thoughts. Your mind is clear, calm. You are feeling comfortable and relaxed. Breathe in and out. Breathe in and out. Let your breath soothe you and bring clarity back to your mind.

Breathe in – I let you go.

Breathe out – Relax.

Breathe in – I let you go.

Breathe out – Relax.

Now, I will slowly count to 20. As the numbers increase, you will become more comfortable and comfortable, free of your thoughts. Imagine yourself detaching from them, observing from above, and then flying away. You choose not to be affected by them.

1, 2, 3, 4, 5, 6, 7, 8, 9, 10, 11, 12, 13, 14, 15, 16, 17, 18, 19, 20.

You may open your eyes now. You are free of tension, and your mind is clearer. You are feeling more relaxed. Gently, get used to the surroundings, and continue with your usual activities.

Morning Mood-Boosting Feel-Good Meditation for an Anxiety-Free Day (10 minutes)

Duration: 10 minutes

We all know that stretching yourself physically and being active right after waking up can be quite beneficial for your overall health. But how about some mental stretches? This quick practice will show you that you can start the day the right way and in the right state of mind by just setting 10 minutes aside for meditation.

By putting our focus on something other than our worries and anxieties, we decrease their power and allow the body and mind to relax. Now, let's relax and boost our mood in just 10 minutes.

As usual, find a comfortable position and make sure not to be distracted for 10 minutes. Close your eyes, and sit still.

For starters, we will try and relax by breathing slowly and calmly. Take a deep breath, through your nose, and release it slowly, again, through the nose. As you do so, imagine yourself being surrounded by birds, butterflies, flowers, or being on the beach, on a meadow – whatever gets you in a relaxing mood faster.

I will count to 20, and you will fall deeper and deeper into relaxation. Breathe calmly and focus on positive and feel-good images.

1, 2, 3, 4, 5, 6, 7, 8, 9, 10, 11, 12, 13, 14, 15, 16, 17, 18, 19, 20.

Now that you are more relaxed, scan your body quickly. From your feet all the way up your head. If there is an area that is tense or clenched, see if you can loosen it up and relax.

Feet – relax.

Ankles – relax.

Lower legs – relax.

Knees – relax.

Upper legs – relax.

Hips – relax.

Pelvic area – relax.

Abdominal area – relax.

Hands and arms – relax.

Shoulders – relax.

Neck – relax.

Face – relax.

Head – relax.

Your body is now relaxed and loose. Imagine that is made of soft and stretchy material. Imagine your legs stretching, your arms, your torso, your head. Imagine yourself pulling on your body and stretching it like soft rubber or chewing gum. You are now incredibly long. As you are pulling and stretching, you feel your body getting lighter and lighter. You are now lighter like a feather; your arms and legs flapping as if they were wings of a bird.

Focus on this sensation. You are growing taller and taller - your whole body becomes softer and loose. You are relaxed; you feel calm and comfortable. The stretching sensation is oddly soothing. Try to get into this feeling.

Now that you are relaxed, stay at this moment, enjoying your own equilibrium. Breathe slowly and calmly.

1, 2, 3, 4, 5.

As I count to 20, you will focus on your body getting smaller and smaller, returning to its normal size.

1, 2, 3, 4, 5 – you are getting smaller.

8, 9, 10, 11 – slowly unstretching.

14, 15, 16 – almost there.

18, 19, 20.

Take a deep breath and exhale slowly.

Breathe in. Breathe out.

A deep inhale. Exhale slowly.

Now, open your eyes. Acknowledge your surroundings. Your relaxed and stress-free day can start now.

Quick After-Work Stress-Relieving Meditation (10 minutes)

<u>Duration: 10 minutes</u>

We usually carry the tension and stress from the office long after our workday has finished. That makes us anxious, nervous, and prevents us from enjoying some quality time with family and friends.

This quick 10-minute meditation will make sure that your work-related thoughts and emotions stay locked away until your next shift. By bringing your focus back to reality and the things that happen around you, you will de-stress and get rid of anxiety that has piled up during your work hours.

You can do this while at the office, as well. You don't need to keep your eyes close, nor to take a certain position. Just make sure that you are sitting comfortably, and that no one will barge in to interrupt your practice.

Take a deep breath and release it slowly through your nose.

A deep inhale. A slow exhale.

Breathe in.

Breathe out.

Feel the tension in your muscles decrease. Soften those areas that feel the tensest, and get loose. Lower your arms and shoulders, soften your belly.

Now, let's drag your attention away from your work and place it onto some concrete things that affect you personally, and at this very moment.

Look around you and acknowledge the people and things that surround you. Do not get into many details at this point, just know they are there.

Next, focus on what you can hear. Are there loud noises? Are you sitting in silence? Make sure to note the sounds and just know that they are there. How do these sounds make you feel?

Focus on your clothes. What are you wearing? Do you have socks on or not? How do your feet feel? How does the material of the clothes make you feel? Are you comfortable? Is your work shirt wrapped tightly around your neckline? Maybe you cannot wait for you to take your uniform off and jump into your casual, comfy clothes. Even if this feels like a negative feeling, focus on it. Think about how good it will feel to get home and relax.

Away from your workplace. Away from your work problems.

Now place your hands on your knees or thighs, and gently run your fingertips over. Focus on the warmth underneath, the fraction between your clothes and fingers. Keep rubbing nd breathe calmly.

I will now count to 20, and as the numbers increase, you will become more and more relaxed. Ready to go home. Ready to enjoy the rest of your day. Away from stress. Away from anxiety.

1, 2, 3, 4, 5, 6, 7, 8, 9, 10, 11, 12, 13, 14, 15, 16, 17, 18, 19, 20.

Now, you are relaxed. You are calm. You are feeling comfortable and ready to perform other activities with a peaceful mind. You can go back to your usual activities now. If distress finds its way back into your mind, simply shift your attention back to the present and how your surroundings make you feel.

Conclusion

Congratulations! You have just gone through 5 hours of meditation. Each of these practices addresses a unique issue, but they will all help you relax, relieve yourself from anxiety, soothe your mind, purge unwanted thoughts away, as well as destroy symptoms of the blues and depression.

Keep in mind, though, that it is the practice that makes perfect. To really enjoy what meditation offers, you need to do it regularly. And while each of these excellent scripts will help you relax and unwind at the moment of practicing, to enjoy the long-term benefits, you will have to make meditating a habit.

So, keep on practicing, and a ticket to the never-stopping journey of tranquility is guaranteed!

www.ingramcontent.com/pod-product-compliance
Lightning Source LLC
Chambersburg PA
CBHW052357060726
47592CB00019B/1380